THE SELF-DEFENSE HANDBOOK

THE BEST STREET FIGHTING MOVES AND SELF-DEFENSE TECHNIQUES

SAM FURY

Illustrated by
NEIL GERMIO

WARNINGS AND DISCLAIMERS

CONTENTS

WEAPON DISARMS

INTRODUCTION

"I fear not the man who has practiced 10,000 kicks one time, but I fear the man who has practiced one kick 10,000 times." - Bruce Lee

This no-nonsense self-defense training manual focuses on the most effective techniques from a wide variety of martial arts, including (but not limited to):

- Jeet Kune Do (Bruce Lee's martial art)
- Vortex Control Self-Defense (eclectic self-defense)
- Kali/Escrima Arnis (Filipino weapon-based martial arts)
- Wing Chun (efficient Chinese martial art)
- Krav Maga (Israeli military)
- Systema (Russian military)
- Mixed martial arts (strikes and ground fighting)

Despite the wide variety of resources, the manual is minimalistic. It contains step-by-step progressive lessons, split into four sections. For best results, learn each section in order.

Section 1: Self-Defense Principles

Explanations of subjects that relate to self-defense and training, but that are not specific techniques.

Section 2: Basic Self-Defense Techniques

Simple and effective techniques allowing you to escape your attacker(s) and get help.

Section 3: Advanced Strikes & Strategies

Essential strikes and basic strategies for self-defense in an ongoing fight. These techniques are also good for when the basic self-defense techniques are too aggressive, such as in a "friendly" pub or school-yard brawl.

Section 4: Weapon Disarms

This section covers weapon disarms with and without your own weapon, as well as group fighting strategy and basic compliance locks.

PRINCIPLES OF SELF-DEFENSE

This section covers generic subjects relating to self-defense that are not techniques.

Do not dismiss the subjects in this section. The information you'll learn here is more valuable from a self-defense point of view than any of the individual techniques.

AWARENESS AND ACTION

Awareness and action give you the best chance of avoiding or surviving any dangerous situation. Here, they are explained in reference to self-defense.

Awareness

Constant awareness of your surroundings and people is the best way to stay out of danger.

You'll notice early warning signs and give off an air of awareness, making you less of a target to attackers.

Whenever you enter a new situation/room, do a scan and take mental note of the following:

- Exits
- Improvised weapons (see Improvised Weapons chapter)
- "Shady" individuals
- Any other potential dangers

Here are some common signs of aggression:

- Stares and/or wide-eyed looks
- Puffed chests
- Sudden/erratic movements
- Verbal threats
- Rowdiness
- Clenched fists
- Displaying a weapon

Action

Decisive action will keep you safe in the face of danger.

Avoidance of a physical conflict is your primary goal when confronted by an aggressive individual. Back up out of striking distance and adopt the passive ready stance (see Ready Stance chapter).

Try one of the following tactics:

- **Defuse.** Keep calm and appear agreeable and friendly. Be polite and co-operative but not too submissive.
- **Comply.** Material goods are usually not worth the fight.
- **Bluff.** Feigning insanity, seizure, or telling a probable attacker you have an infectious disease may deter him.

When your avoidance tactic doesn't work, you'll need to choose between flight or fight.

"Flight" translates to "run and scream." It is always preferred over fighting.

If applicable, throw what your attacker wants in the direction opposite the one you want to run.

Run to a safe place—a well-lit area where there are other people, such as a police station, gas station, or mall.

If you're hiding, call the police, then put your phone on silent.

When forced to fight, be aggressive and run when possible.

Movement will save your life. Struggle, strike, run.

Note: If your initial fight isn't successful and it's clear you'll be taken, surrender before you're knocked out, killed, or otherwise incapacitated.

Learn escape and evasion techniques to give you the best chance of survival beyond the initial fight.

www.SurvivalFitnesslan.com/Evading-Escaping-Capture

After an Attack

The following tips will keep you safe after an attack:

- Flee the area to a safe place.
- Call emergency services.
- Apply emergency first aid.
- Seek medical attention even if you have no visible injuries.
- Do not drive, in case you experience delayed shock.
- Write down a description of your attackers and the incident, including how they got away (on foot, type of vehicle, direction, etc.)
- Cancel credit cards, if applicable.
- Change your locks if your keys were stolen.
- If someone calls to tell you they found your stuff, get someone else to pick it up while you stay home.
- Join support groups if you feel the need to do so.

Reasonable Force

Different situations call for different degrees of force. It's up to you to decide.

Do what you need to do to escape, but know that your actions have consequences. If you're excessive, you may get in trouble with the law.

If you're confronted by the police in a situation where excessive force may be an issue, stay quiet. Be polite, but only tell them whatever is required by law in your country, such as your name and address. Never admit any wrongdoing, and get a lawyer.

PRINCIPLES OF ATTACK

When you have to fight, attack is your best defense.

Follow these four principles to ensure your attack is successful.

Surprise

There are several ways to harness the element of surprise.

Strike first. When you feel that violence is unavoidable, you have a much better chance of coming out on top if you land the first blow. But don't stop there—keep attacking until your assailant is down. The first blow is not enough. You want the last blow as well.

Strike when he is distracted. Striking first is good. Striking when he isn't ready is better.

All you need is half a second for him to look away, blink, or have a thought.

You can create this time by asking him a question, striking low, making a random noise, etc.

Simplicity

As with many things in life, keeping things simple is the best way to obtain your objective.

In self-defense, your objective is to escape.

A few simple strikes to primary target areas will get you out of most situations so you can run away.

Aggression

Attack hard, fast, and unrelentingly until you achieve your objective.

A good strike may knock him out, but don't expect it. Continue to attack until you have done enough damage to give you time to get away.

You must also be aggressive in an escape. Whether you choose to run or fight, to retreat or close in, do it wholeheartedly. In a self-defense situation, hesitation is your enemy.

Adaptation

Every situation is different, and every action has a reaction.

If something doesn't work, try a different approach.

Keep moving, keep attacking, and keep struggling until you're free.

One of the main reasons simple strikes are better than "fancy" self-defense techniques is because they are easy to adapt.

TARGET AREAS

To get the most "bang for your buck," hit as hard as you can in the most vulnerable area available. That isn't necessarily a pressure point. You do not need a pinpoint hit. This is what makes the areas below good targets.

Primary Targets

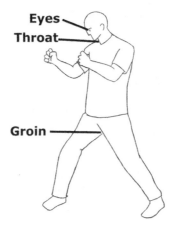

Attacking one of these areas will cause high pain with little effort (except for applying a chokehold, which is an advanced technique).

Eyes. A small but very vulnerable area. Use an eye gouge.

Neck/Throat. Cause pain or choke your attacker out. Press into the hollow point below his Adam's apple with your thumb, or apply a chokehold.

Groin. Attacking the groin is effective on all genders. Kick, knee, grab, etc.

Secondary Targets

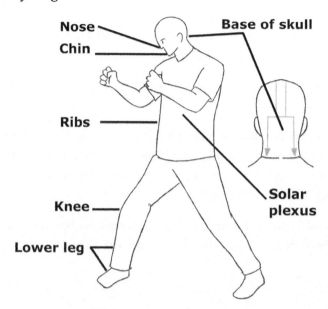

When you do not want to cause so much damage, or if a primary target isn't available, one of these secondary target areas can get the job done.

Base of Skull. Although you need to be behind him, a good elbow or palm heel to the base of his skull can knock someone out.

Nose. A strike to this soft target will cause pain, the attacker's eyes will water, and there will be high potential for blood flow (which is psychologically damaging).

Point of Chin. A good strike here can knock someone out, especially if his mouth is open (strike while he's talking). Use palm heels, elbows, knees, and punches.

Solar Plexus. A solid rear elbow, knee, or straight punch to the solar plexus will knock the wind out of him.

Ribs. His lower ribs are a great lower torso/side target. Use shovel hooks and/or horizontal elbow strikes.

Knee. A side kick to the knee will stop an advancing attacker in his tracks. It also has the potential to end the fight.

Lower leg. A kick to the shin or stomp on the foot are great pain distractions.

The target areas above are preferred, but not exclusive. Hitting almost anywhere is better than nowhere, as long the target area isn't harder than your weapon. For example, don't punch your attacker in the forehead.

Notable hard points in the body are the upper part of the head (above the eyebrow/temple line), the elbows, and the knees.

TRAINING

None of the techniques in this manual will work without training.

You can learn every technique in this book in one day if you want to, but that is not enough to gain skill.

Here is my advice (and how I train myself and others).

First, go through the techniques one by one, in order. If you learn five to six techniques a day, it will take about a week.

After that, have a training daily session. The session might include some or all of the following:

- Warm up
- Technique training
- Reaction training
- Conditioning/fitness
- Cool down/stretch
- Box breathing

When you're confident, teach others. This has a number of benefits:

- It lets you show your loved ones how to protect themselves
- It gives you training partners
- It helps you absorb the lessons more fully

Safety in Training

Here are some tips to promote a safe training session:

- Ensure you are physically ready before you begin training. If you have any doubts, see your physician.
- Use proper equipment where applicable, such as mats, training weapons, and protective clothing.

- Wear safety equipment, but fight as if you do not have it so you do not become careless with your defense.
- Remove all jewelry.
- Don't train with injuries. If you are injured, get injuries checked out by a professional ASAP to prevent them from getting worse.
- Train for reality, but use only enough force to get the desired effect.
- Tap out early.

Tapping Out

Tapping out is something you can do when you want to submit/give up—when a lock starts to hurt, for example. Tap your opponent at least twice, so that he feels it. He must disengage immediately. If you cannot reach your opponent, tap the floor. You can also use a verbal tap-out, such as "stop."

Put safety before pride. "Tap out" before you need to.

Warm Up

Prepare your body for exercise with light physical movement. This prevents injury during harder training.

Doing 5 to 10 superburpees is good. A superburpee is a warm up, muscle conditioner, and stretching exercise all in one. Instructions on how to do superburpees are in your bonus materials (see the Bonus Materials chapter at the end of this manual).

Five to 10 minutes of jogging, skipping, or light shadowboxing are also good options.

Technique

Choose one or two techniques to concentrate on in each training session.

Train yourself in each technique to increase your force, speed, and accuracy.

Go slowly to start, focusing on correct movement. Ensure you stay balanced throughout. You want to instill correct movement in your muscle memory. Do this via repetition.

Poorly trained movement is hard to unlearn, so do it correctly from the start. Use a mirror.

Once you have the right movement, increase speed. Stay relaxed and move smoothly. Only tense up on impact.

One thing that will help increase your speed is to minimize telegraphing. Telegraphing is any preparatory movement you make that can alert the opponent to your intended action.

Pulling your hand back, looking at a target area, or twitching your face are all examples of telegraphing. You want to telegraph as little as possible to ensure maximum speed and surprise. Train yourself to strike from wherever your hand (or foot) happens to be.

To read signs your opponent might be telegraphing, look at his chest or eyes. Looking at his chest is less confrontational.

Always imagine a target area when you're training, whether you're striking a pad or the air. Aim for the target and snap through it to increase force.

Finally, practice your strikes with full force against a punching bag or partner-held pads. This type of training:

- Conditions your body to absorb the impact of strikes.

- Allows you to use full aggression by combining intensity with force.
- Helps to prevent you from pulling back strikes in a real situation.

Lead/Rear Sides

Your lead side is whichever side of your body is furthest forward and your rear side is whichever side of your body is furthest back.

For example, if you're in a right-foot-forward stance, then your right side is your lead side and your left side is your rear side.

In most cases, it's preferable to have your dominant side as your lead and to strike with it. However, you should always train on both sides of your body.

A lead strike is not as powerful as a rear strike because there's less momentum, but it's less telegraphed. Train to improve the power of your lead strikes.

Reaction Training

Reaction training is when you react to an unknown attack. Your training partner(s) attack you, and you defend yourself/escape in whatever way you want. This type of training allows you to:

- Figure out what works best for you.
- Learn how to adapt techniques to various situations.
- Instill the "act fast" mindset.

Start slowly. As your skills improve, increase your speed in a safe manner.

The key to this type of training is to attack and react as much like you would in a real scenario as possible while still staying safe (that is, not giving yourself lasting injuries). For example, an attacker is unlikely to grab you and stay still. Expect him to have the intention of dragging you away.

Your power level is separate from your intensity. You can still act very aggressively while not actually hitting your training partner.

Expect some pain and bruises. These are good in moderation, as they ensure you won't be shocked by impact in a real-life situation.

Vary your training partners so you get different reactions, sizes, strengths, etc.

Conditioning/Fitness

Fighting takes a lot of energy.

Basic self-defense training with warm up, technique, and reaction training will keep you fit, but the longer you can last, the better chance you'll have.

Also, your number one defense is to run, so training to outrun your opponent is very useful.

Sprinting is an excellent way to do this. Work your way up to sprinting non-stop for longer and longer periods of time.

Circuit training with sprints, pushups, and other conditioning exercises (pullups, superburpees, etc.) makes an excellent no-equipment workout.

Cool Down/Stretching

Stretching your body ensures your muscles stay supple. This increases flexibility and speed in movement. It also promotes faster muscle recovery and prevents injury.

Box Breathing

Box breathing is a simple breathing technique created by Mark Divine. Use it to calm yourself in stressful situations.

- Empty your lungs of all air.
- Hold for four seconds.
- Inhale through your nose for four seconds.
- Hold for four seconds.
- Exhale for four seconds.
- Repeat several times if needed.

Practice box breathing for a minimum of five minutes at the end of your training session. This simple form of meditation will lower your overall stress levels, which will keep you calmer in stressful situations.

BASIC SELF-DEFENSE
TECHNIQUES

Use the techniques in this section to escape potentially life-threatening situations such as abduction and sexual assault. These are
things every man, woman, and child should know for self-defense.

READY STANCE

The ready stance ensures balance and accessibility of movement for attack and defense. You can adjust it to convey a passive or an aggressive demeanor depending on the message you want to send your opponent.

As soon as you feel threatened, take up the ready stance.

In the case of a surprise attack, take it up when you can.

Passive Ready Stance

Use the passive ready stance when you're unsure if a confrontation will turn violent, and/or to give the impression of compliance.

Step back with your weak leg so your feet are shoulder width apart. Stepping back is non-aggressive gesture and creates space.

Bend your knees slightly and hold your hands up at eye level, shoulder-width apart.

Turn your palms towards your opponent, facing slightly inward and aiming at his head.

Keep your elbows close to your body.

Relax your muscles so you can make faster movements when needed.

Aggressive Ready Stance

The aggressive ready stance is a more compact version of the passive ready stance.

Adopt it from the start if you expect violence, or after the first strike from you or your opponent.

Lean forward slightly, with a more prominent lead hand.

Tuck your elbows closer to your body, and drop your hip so you're facing him more side-on.

Keep your teeth together, but not tightly clenched, and tuck your chin behind your lead shoulder.

Close your hands into loose fists if you want.

Stay relaxed.

When adopting the aggressive ready stance from the outset (not after a passive ready stance) you can either step back with your weak leg (for example, when you're pushed) or lunge forward with your dominant leg as you attack.

Do not step forward without an attack or defensive counter. Doing so makes you easier to strike.

FOOTWORK

Correct footwork allows you to move while staying balanced.

The ready stance gives you the base for proper footwork. No matter where you move, keep as close to the ready stance as possible.

General principles:

- Take small steps. Several small steps are better than one big one.
- Keep your feet low to the ground and shoulder-width apart.
- Keep your feet under your body, with your knees slightly bent and your guard up.
- Never cross your feet.
- Move smoothly.
- Whichever way you're moving, that is the foot that moves first. For example, if you're moving forward, move your front foot first. If you're moving right, move your right foot first.

Forward Shuffle

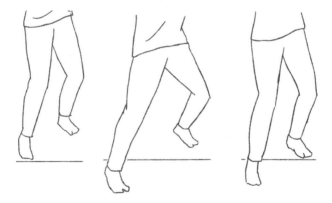

When your opponent is too far away for your attack to be effective, move your body closer with the forward shuffle. Overreaching with your strike lessens its impact and puts you off balance.

From the ready stance, move your front foot forward about half a step. Slide your rear foot up to take your front foot's original position.

Glide on the balls of your feet, with your weight spread as evenly as possible over your legs.

Repeat this motion to advance further.

Rear Shuffle

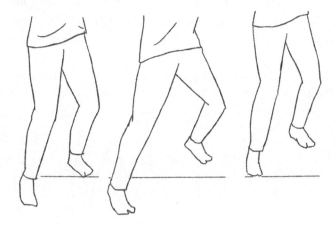

The rear shuffle is the opposite of the forward shuffle.

Move your rear foot back about half a step and place your front foot in your rear foot's original position.

As you slide your front foot back, your weight will momentarily shift to your stationary rear foot. Keep your rear heel raised.

Repeat the motion to retreat as far as needed.

Moving backwards is not recommended in a self-defense situation. Running away is, but that is not moving backwards. You should turn and run.

There are two major problems with moving backwards:

- It goes against the "crowding your opponent" principle (see Blitzkrieg).
- You don't know what is behind you.

However, there are some circumstances in which it's necessary, such as when you need to time an interception (see slip, parry, and strike) or to evade multiple attackers.

You can strike with a rear shuffle, but it won't be a forceful blow. If you want it to be effective, stop your retreat and shift your weight slightly forward to make an offensive strike before continuing backwards.

Side Steps

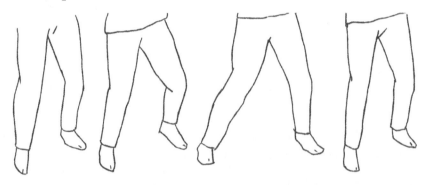

Assuming you want to move to the right, move your right foot half a step in that direction. Immediately move your left foot to the right to re-adopt the ready stance.

All Other Directions

Perform circular and diagonal movements in the same fashion. Keep to the general principles, and you'll be able to go in any direction you need to.

IMPROVISED WEAPONS

When running isn't an option, and you have the opportunity to get one, use a weapon.

If you can hit with, thrust, throw, spray, or hide behind something, it's a potential improvised weapon. That covers almost any object, though some are better than others.

A good improvised weapon is one that you can carry around without suspicion—that is, one a police officer would not take off you in the street. Examples of such weapons are:

- An umbrella
- A pen
- Hairspray and a lighter (for a makeshift flamethrower)

There are four types of improvised weapons that are the best to use for self-defense:

- Knives
- Clubs
- Shields
- Projectiles

When training with improvised weapons, choose things you routinely carry around, like an umbrella, a pen, or trade tools.

The generic grip for any weapon is to hold it firmly in your fist, but not so tightly that doing so causes fatigue. Put your legs in an aggressive ready stance.

Knives

Knives are one-handed thrusting objects. Besides an actual knife, you could use a bottle, scissors, a rolled-up magazine, etc.

Hold the knife in your strong hand and use a weak lead.

Position your knife hand down and back at your waist. Use your lead hand to guard.

Thrust straight out at your opponent's abdomen and bring your arm straight back

Clubs

A club can be any solid object that is too big to be a knife, but not so big that it's cumbersome. A metal pipe, a baseball bat, a walking stick, etc., are all good clubs.

Hold your club in both hands, up behind your shoulder. Alternatively, hold it in one hand and use the other as a guard.

Strike straight down into your opponent's head, and/or thrust the club into his face or gut. You can also strike his knee, which is a less damaging target, but will still put him out of commission.

Shields

Anything you can hide behind or use as an obstacle—a chair, a door, a wall, a backpack, etc.— makes a good shield.

If you can pick it up, use it to block and thrust. If it's an immovable object, ram your opponent's head into it.

Projectiles

A projectile is anything you can throw or spray that isn't better used some other way, such as an ashtray, deodorant, hot liquid, or dirt.

Tactical Pen

A tactical pen is a good example of a knife weapon that you can carry around without suspicion. The best type of tactical pen for self-defense is one that you'll carry. Any simple stainless-steel pen will work, but ideally, you'll choose one that:

- Is refillable
- Writes well (you like it)
- Has a clip
- Has a flat top (that won't stab you)
- Is easy to replace/inexpensive
- Can pass as a normal pen (to get through security)

Most of the tactical pens on the market do not fill these requirements, especially the last one. Those that do include:

- Zebra 701
- Zebra 402
- Parker Jotter
- Fisher Space Military Pen (this one is a little more expensive, but still under $20)

Clip your tactical pen somewhere on your body that is easy to access with your dominant hand, such as your front pants pocket on your dominant side. Put it in the same place every time and practice deploying it, so doing so becomes second nature.

When you grab the pen, hold it in an icepick grip, with your thumb on top.

Every time you initially grab the pen, including to write something or to put it away, use this grip.

Grab the pen and thrust it straight into your opponent in one swift movement. A cardboard box makes a good target when training.

You can strike from almost any angle. Thrust the pen into any target area to help you escape.

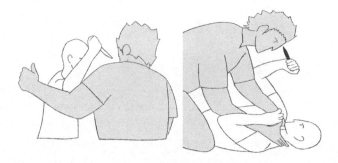

Sap

Anything heavy in a sock makes a good improvised sap. You can use coins, a billiard ball, a soda can, or a rock.

Another way to make one is to tie a metal nut (or something similar) to a piece of cord, such as a shoelace.

A piece of material about the size of a tea towel (or t-shirt) with a small weighted object (like a handful of coins) in it also works.

- Put the object in the center of the material.
- Fold the material diagonally in half over the object.
- Roll up the material from the point to the base.

Hold both ends so the object in the middle is now the striking end. Use it like a club—that is, make vertical strikes to your opponent's head. You can also uppercut.

LOW SIDE-KICK

The low side-kick has a number of advantages over a hand strike:

- Greater reach
- More power
- Hard to defend against
- Unexpected attack
- Multi-directional

A low side-kick to your opponent's lead shin or knee uses your longest weapon on the closest target. The shin and knee are also hard for your opponent to protect. This makes the kick an excellent option for a first strike.

The leg closest to your target is your kicking leg. Lift your foot off the ground and thrust the bottom of it into your opponent's shin or knee.

Lean away from him as you kick, and keep your stationary leg a little bent. This balances you and creates distance from your upper body. Do all of this in one smooth motion.

Use the low side-kick in any direction to stop an advancing opponent and/or to divert his attention before an escape. A solid side-kick to the knee can be a fight finisher.

Even if your opponent has a weapon (not a gun), the low side-kick is useful. It keeps you at a distance and can buy you precious seconds to escape.

When you put your foot down, shift your weight so you're facing your attacker, ready for a follow-up strike.

An adaptation of the low side-kick is the back heel/stomp. Use this when you're grabbed tightly from behind—in a bear hug, for example. Do the closest thing to a low side-kick that you can.

Improve your ability to balance on one leg by standing on one foot while doing different tasks, such as putting on your clothes or washing the dishes.

GROIN ATTACK

There are many ways to attack the groin, and when it's open, it's an excellent target.

Groin Grab

When your hands are pinned down, grab your opponent's groin and squeeze or twist.

The groin grab is also useful on the ground. Here is it combined with the eye gouge.

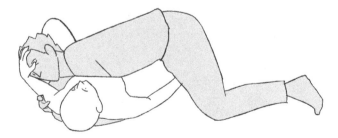

Groin Kick

Swing your foot straight up, like you're kicking a football. As a general rule, never kick higher than the groin. Kicking low will help you keep your balance.

Groin Knee

When you're close to your opponent, lift your knee straight up into his groin.

Groin Strike

A groin strike can be in any direction and with any weapon. Groin kicks and knees are examples of types of groin strikes. In this image it is to the rear with a forearm.

FINGER-BENDING

When striking isn't enough to make an attacker let you go, attack his fingers. Grab two of his fingers in one hand and two in the other. Pull them apart.

When you can't get this grip, go for any single finger you can and bend/twist it back towards his wrist. The little/pinky finger is easiest to manipulate.

PALM HEEL

A palm heel is a good striking weapon. Use it to prevent damage to your knuckles.

Bend the top part of your fingers down and your wrist back. Hold your thumb against your fingers.

Strike up under your attacker's chin with the lower part of your palm.

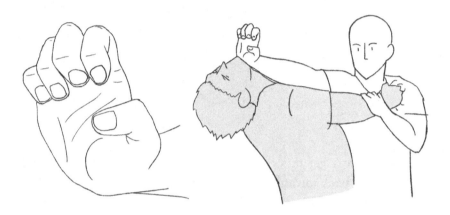

ELBOWS

The elbow is an excellent striking weapon for close combat. It's the hardest point on your body, you can get a lot of power behind it, and it's effective from a variety of angles.

When throwing an elbow strike, keep your hand open to expose the bone. Pin your thumb to your chest as you snap it into your target. Generate power with a pivot in your hips.

Increase the force behind the strike by grabbing your opponent's head and pulling it into your elbow as you strike.

Your elbow is also a good option for a rear strike to the body or head.

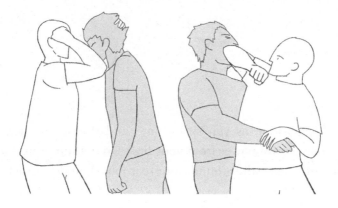

ELBOW BURST

The elbow burst is a simultaneous attack and defense. It covers your head, face, and throat with your arms, and protects your arteries with your forearms.

A sudden forward movement crowds your opponent, which lessens the impact of his strike. At the same time, your elbow is driven into him to cause pain and drive him back.

The elbow burst is effective against a surprise attack from the front when you're too close to use a side-kick. You can deploy it from a casual standing position, such as with your feet shoulder-width apart, or from the ready stance.

To do the elbow burst, place your lead palm on the top of your head, with the tip of your elbow pointing straight forward. Tuck your chin into your lead shoulder. Keep your eyes up and teeth together. Put your rear palm on the side of your head/ear.

Adopt this position as you spring into and through your attacker using the explosive power from your legs. Do not jump up. Your feet should hardly leave the ground. Your rear foot should skim across it.

You'll land in a deeper stance due to the explosiveness of the movement. Adopt the aggressive ready position as you continue to attack or run away.

The hand position used in the elbow burst is also a good defensive "cover up" position. Use it when you're getting dominated by a flurry of strikes.

Hold your forearms towards the direction of attack and back out to run away.

When you can't back out, close in on your attacker to nullify some of the power behind his strikes, and attack his eyes, groin, etc.

If you're on the ground, tuck your legs up to protect yourself further, and stay on your back until you can bring him down (see Ground Takedown chapter).

EYE GOUGE

The eye is a small target, but if you get to it, you can disable most attackers. Dig your thumb into it as hard as you need to.

Doing this is also an effective ground defense.

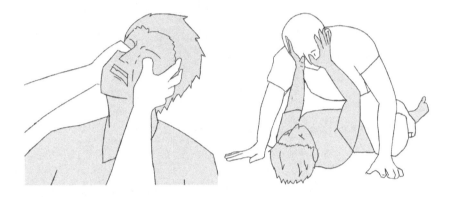

When you don't want to do something so violent, apply the same technique to the hollow in your attacker's throat or the indent behind the bottom of his ear lobe.

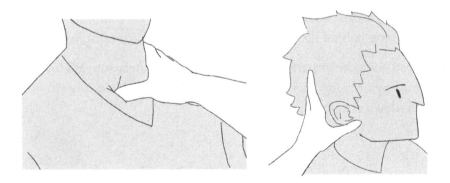

HEADBUTT

A headbutt is a last-resort strike. Doing it may disorient you, so make sure you push your forehead into a soft target, such as your opponent's nose. Make contact using the area 3 cm (1 in) above your eyebrow. Keep your teeth together and your chin tucked.

BREAKFALLS

Whether you're pushed, tripped, thrown, or you fall, a breakfall will lessen the impact.

The side breakfall is the most common, but it's important to learn the front and back breakfalls as well.

The technique for each is different, but there are two major things to look out for:

- Do not stick your hand down. This is a natural reaction, but taking the impact of the fall on a single point will cause injury.
- Protect your head by angling it away from the ground as you land.

Practice your breakfalls on a soft-but-firm surface, such as grass or a gym mat. Do it often, so they become instinctive.

Once you're proficient, train yourself in doing breakfalls in realistic scenarios, such as when you're pushed or thrown to the ground.

Side Breakfall

From a standing position, step forward with your right leg and do a single-leg squat as you bring your left leg through.

The more you bend the leg, the closer you'll be to the ground before landing.

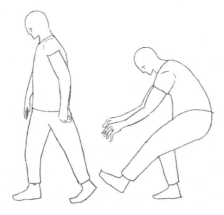

Get as low to the ground as you can, tuck your chin to your chest, and fall onto the left side of your torso/back. You'll also land on the whole of your left arm, which should be splayed out about 45 degrees from your body, palm facing down. Breathe out as you hit the ground. Your legs will probably go in the air.

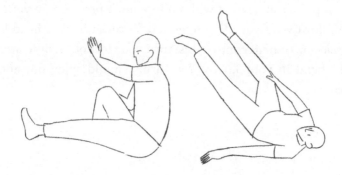

Allow your legs to come back to the ground in a position where they are comfortable, but not crossed or splayed too widely.

Back Breakfall

Squat down as low as you can and tuck your chin to your chest.

Fall onto your back and arms. Don't roll back too much.

If you stop the roll dead, it will put too much pressure on your body, but you don't want your legs to go too far towards your head for the same reason. To help control this, turn your feet out a little and keep a slight bend in your knees. Your arms should splay out about 45 degrees.

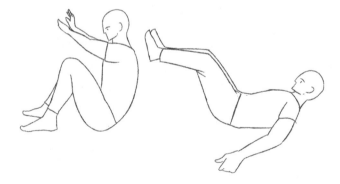

Forward Breakfall

With the front breakfall, you fall directly forward and land on your forearms.

Start on your knees so you're low to the ground. Put your arms in front of your face in an upside-down V.

As you fall towards the ground, tense your core, and take the impact on your forearms. Try not to let your belly hit the ground.

Turn your face to the side if you have time (not pictured).

Once you're confident, do it from a standing position. Spread your legs so you can be lower to the ground.

Eventually, you'll be able to do it from a full standing position.

KICK AND PIVOT

When you end up on the ground, use a kick-and-pivot to protect yourself.

Swing your feet to face your attacker. Use one arm to defend yourself and one leg to kick him if he comes towards you. Pivot as he moves to keep your feet pointed towards him.

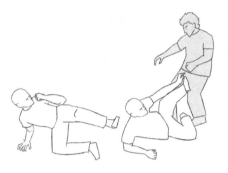

Getting Up

From the kick-and-pivot position, use your other hand and foot to scoot away until you have enough distance to get up.

Swing your feet behind you so that they are close to the ready position. Use one hand to push yourself up off the ground and the other to protect your face.

Stand up and adopt the ready position.

Dead Weight

Although going to the ground is not normally advised, it's a good way to buy time in an abduction situation where you know you can't fight off your attacker.

When you're grabbed, fall to the ground and become a dead weight.

Scream for help as you kick and pivot.

This is a good default move for children who are too small to fight off adults. They should scream, "Help, this is a stranger!" In a public setting, this will often be enough to make the attacker flee the scene.

APPLICATION

This section demonstrates how you can apply the attacks taught so far in realistic scenarios.

Most of these scenarios assume an attacker is abducting you. He is grabbing and taking you. When you can escape from these holds with the intent of movement, you can also escape them from stationary positions. This isn't always true the other way around.

These three pointers will get you out of most holds:

- Act fast. Strike and struggle to get free.
- Attack his fingers if needed.
- Run as soon as possible.

Here are some additional tips for when your simple strikes are not working.

Chokes

With any choke, your first priority is to free your airway.

Adopt the elbow-burst position as best as you can.

Slide your hands down your head and hook them down hard on your attacker's forearm, preferably at his wrist.

As soon as a gap is a created, tuck your chin to your shoulder.

Attack and struggle to get your head out.

As a last resort, bite him. Shaking your head while you bite will cause more pain.

For a front choke, if the above doesn't work, arch your back to bring your head up and away from your attacker. Place your hands on his hips if you need to.

Move your head across his belly to free it.

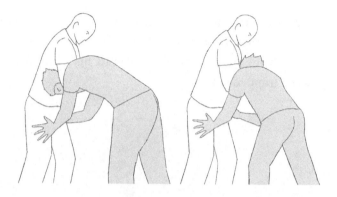

Getting Pulled

When pulling against an attacker isn't working, close in to attack and then pull away again.

Lifted

Hook your leg around your attacker to prevent him from lifting you too high.

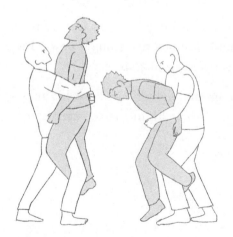

Mount Position

The mount position is when you're on your back on the ground and your attacker is on top of you. To get out of this position, hook one of your feet around the outside of his and grab his arm on the same side. This is the trapped side.

Buck your hips to direct him forward and over to the side you trapped. This will flip him over so you're on top.

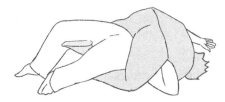

Strike him a few times and get to your feet. To prevent yourself from hitting the ground, do not strike straight down. Instead, use hooking elbows, an eye gouge, a groin grab, etc.

An experienced ground fighter may cross his ankles around you and try to pull you in. Push on his torso to create distance.

Use stiff arms for support and attack his groin with your knee.

A last resort is to smash the back of his head on the ground. This will knock most people out, but can cause brain damage or death.

ADVANCED STRIKES & STRATEGIES

The fighting tactics in this section are good to use when you're in an ongoing fight and/or when the basic techniques are too aggressive.

LEAD STRAIGHT PUNCH

The lead straight punch is fast, accurate, powerful, and practical.

From the ready position, whip your fist straight out into your target from the center of your body. Do not pull back before you strike.

Your rear hand should be up as you throw the strike for defense and/or counter-attack.

For maximum reach and power, allow your weight to shift over your front leg as you twist your hip and extend your shoulder. Do not allow your elbow to lock straight. This will limit your power, and may cause you to injure yourself.

Do not lean back while punching, but don't lean too far forward either. If you need to get closer, use footwork to close the distance.

As your strike makes contact, snap your wrist and clench your hand into a vertical fist, with your thumb up and knuckles pointed toward your target.

Your bottom three knuckles will make contact as you snap your fist through your target. This is not a push.

Allow your arm to come back to the ready stance naturally, either straight back or elliptically. Do not let it drop down, as that leaves an opening.

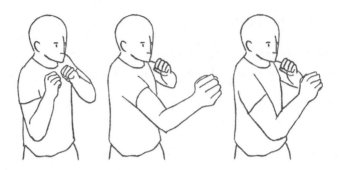

Combining the lead straight with a forward shuffle allows you to close ground and increase power.

Here, your hand moves first, with your lead foot following closely. To the observer, these movements will look simultaneous, but you must move your hand first to prevent telegraphing.

Your fist should your target before your foot lands; otherwise, you'll lose power. This is true for all hand strikes. In all foot techniques, the foot moves first.

Forming a Fist

A proper fist will allow you to punch without injuring yourself.

Hold your hand out flat, with your fingers together and your thumb up.

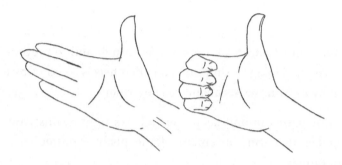

Roll your fingers into your palm and then bring your thumb down over your fingers.

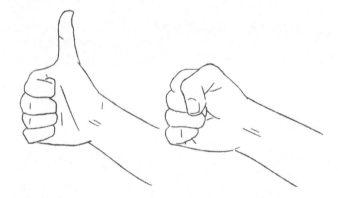

Hold your fist loosely until just before it makes contact. You need to have relaxed muscles to produce speed and power. This is true for all strikes.

The alignment of your wrist is important to all punches. Angle your wrist up to align your fist with your forearm. If your first connects while your wrist is bent down, you will get injured.

As long as you hold your fist correctly, you can strike from any angle.

Condition your knuckles for a stronger punch and to prevent injury while striking. Doing pushups on clenched fists is a good way to start. Do them with your wrists aligned as described.

Point your palms in and keep your elbows tight against your body. This makes the arm movement of the pushup mimic that of the straight punch.

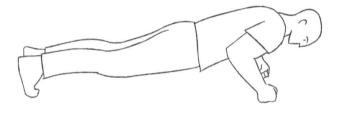

SLIP, PARRY, AND STRIKE

The slip, parry, and strike technique is a combination of three techniques that you can use for defense or as an opening gambit.

You can do each technique individually, or use any two together without the third. For example, you can:

- Slip and parry
- Slip and strike
- Parry and strike

If you need to close a distance for your strike to connect, incorporate a forward shuffle.

Slipping

Slipping is an evasive technique used against a straight punch (jab, cross, lead straight, etc.). It allows you to evade a strike, stay in striking range, and have both hands free to counter-attack.

As an attack comes in, move your head to the outside of the attacker's striking arm and a little forward. Move only as much as is needed not to get hit. Timing and spatial judgment are the key factors.

You can slip to either side of the attacker's guard.

Parrying

Parrying is a quick hand motion used to deflect blows away from you. It's preferred to blocking, which uses force to stop a blow. In parrying, timing and economy of motion are important, not force.

Only parry when needed and at the last possible moment. Only move as much as needed to deflect a strike and/or to create openings for counters. Your parry should not go past your shoulder.

When you're parrying, your elbow should stay relatively fixed while you use your hand and arm to make the movement.

Most of the time, you'll parry with your rear hand, which will leave your lead free to counter, but parrying with your lead is also possible.

When you're using the slip and parry together, the slip is your main defensive maneuver. The parry is a backup, and may not make contact. You can parry by moving your hand across your body (pictured) or to the outside.

Slip, Parry, and Strike

Combine the slip and parry with a straight punch.

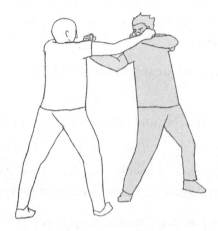

Slipping to the outside is also possible.

1 - 2 COMBINATION

The 1-2 combination is a fundamental boxing combination that uses the jab (1) to set the opponent up/get you in range, and then a cross (2) as the main landing blow.

Here, it's been adapted for you to use with the lead and rear straight punches.

Throw a lead straight and then a rear straight immediately afterwards.

The lead straight goes out with your lead foot. As your rear foot comes up, your lead straight comes in and your rear straight goes out.

The rear straight punch is thrown straight out in front of your nose and hits your target with a snap in your rear shoulder, preferably into the side of your opponent's jaw.

To maximize the force behind the punch, make full use of momentum and drive your body behind the punch. Remember to snap, not push.

The rear straight goes out as the lead straight comes back in, and connects before your rear foot lands. Your lead hand becomes the defensive hand while your rear punch is out.

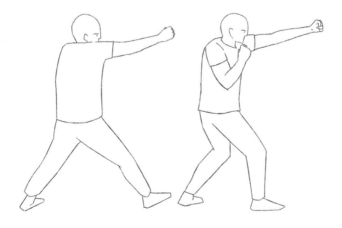

Multiple Straights

You do not have to stop at two straight punches. You can do as many in a row as you want, while shuffling forward to crowd your opponent.

SNAP-BACK

The snap-back is a useful technique for evading a strike to the head. Use it when you're too far away for a slip, parry, and strike, but don't want to do a rear shuffle. As the strike comes in, snap your body out of range and come straight back.

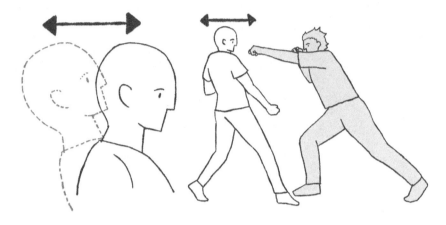

You can also use it with the rear shuffle if needed.

The return from the snap-back is a good time to counter (with a 1-2 combination, for example).

KNEES

Knee strikes are the elbows of your legs. Pull your opponent's head down as you drive your knee up into his face. Point your foot and toes down for protection, and be careful not to lose your balance. Do a few consecutively for more damage.

Defending Against Knees

Adopt the elbow-burst position. It protects your head and drops your elbow into your opponent's thigh.

SHOVEL HOOK

A shovel hook is useful for getting inside your opponent's guard or defending someone who is or tries to clinch (hug) you. It's one of the shortest-range strikes, but has a massive impact when done correctly.

To do it, tuck your elbow in close to your body. If you're aiming for your opponent's body, hold your elbow against your hips. If you're aiming for his head, hold your elbow against your lower ribs.

Form a proper fist (see Lead Straight Punch) and angle it so your palm faces up to the sky at about a 45-degree angle. Twist your body explosively to send your fist into the target. Generate power by pivoting your hips.

Shovel Hook Defense

Drop your elbows to cover your ribs. Move back as the punches come in.

GUILLOTINE

Strikes are generally a more effective way to fight off an attacker than chokeholds.

However, striking a tough opponent continuously will cause you fatigue and/or injury. When your initial flurry of strikes has little effect, a chokehold can help.

It may also be the only option when you're too close to use your elbows and knees.

When applied correctly, the guillotine and other chokeholds can cause unconsciousness within 10 seconds.

Disengage from the chokehold as soon as your opponent goes limp. Continuing to apply it will lead to brain damage and eventually death.

In most cases, your opponent will regain consciousness within 30 seconds, so escape as soon as he's out.

In training, let go as soon as your opponent taps out (see Training).

To apply the guillotine, wrap your arm around the back of your opponent's neck and under the front of it. His head should be to the side of your torso.

Your palm should face your chest, so that the top of your wrist cuts into his throat just below his Adam's apple. Use your other hand to grasp your first hand and pull up into yourself with both hands. Keep your feet in the fighter's stance for balance.

For an alternative grip, place your other hand on his shoulder. Grab your forearm with your first hand and arch your back to apply the chokehold.

Defense Against Being Tackled

A guillotine chokehold is a good counter to the common tackle.

As your opponent comes in, widen your legs and drop your weight on top of him from your center of gravity. You can drop your elbow into his back at the same time, and/or punch him in the ribs.

Apply the guillotine

Guillotine on the Ground

If you lose your balance and end up on the ground, wrap your legs around your opponent and cross your ankles to lock him in.

Push him away with your legs while pulling his neck towards your chin.

REAR NAKED CHOKE

When you're behind your opponent, a rear naked choke (RNC) is a good way to take him out.

Place his trachea is at the crook of your elbow.

If your right arm is around his neck, grab your left bicep with your right hand. Put your left hand behind his head and squeeze your elbows together.

If needed, force him to expose his neck by pulling up at his eyes or scraping your forearm under his nose.

To sneak up on someone (to help a friend, for example), come in below his line of sight. That way, if he turns around, you have a few more moments before he spots you.

Rear Naked Choke on the Ground

When ground fighting, the best position to be in is the rear mount, applying the RNC. In this position, you're on your opponent's back, facing the same way. Both your legs are wrapped around him, with your heels "hooked" inside his legs.

Do not cross your feet.

Apply the RNC.

Improvised Garrote

Applying a rear naked choke correctly isn't easy. An improvised garrote has a much greater chance of success.

Make one out of a shoelace and a couple of pens, or similar items. Tie an overhand loop in each end of the shoelace. Insert pens in the loops to make handles.

Get behind your opponent and loop the cord around his neck. Pull as hard as you can until he's out.

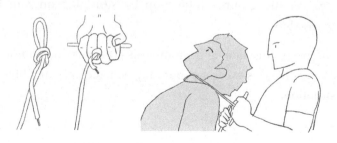

SIMPLE TRIP

Tripping your opponent so he lands on the ground will demoralize him. If he lands incorrectly, it can also cause him injury.

When you're standing, your feet make up two points of a triangle.

The third point, which can be on either side, is one at which you're most off-balance.

When forced towards this third point, you'll become unbalanced, and if you're unable to reposition yourself, you'll fall.

To use this against an opponent, place a foot at the third point of his triangle and use it as a pivot point to shove him to the ground.

Get your foot/leg as close to his body as possible without losing your own balance.

Once he's on the ground, follow up by stomping on him before running to safety.

Come in from the side and stomp his knees, ribs, and/or chest. Stomping his head is excessive, but may be necessary in a life-threatening situation.

GROUND TAKEDOWN

In most cases, being on the ground is bad, and your primary aim is to get back on your feet. Use the kick-and-pivot technique until you have enough space to stand.

If your opponent manages to get around your kick-and-pivot defense, put your hands in the elbow-burst position and bring your knees up.

Do you best to angle your defense towards his attack.

As a kick comes in, or when he gets close enough, grab his leg(s). Get up on one knee and hug his leg(s) tightly at his knee(s). Bring him to the ground by leaning across his thighs and shifting all your weight downward at a diagonal angle.

Stand and attack, and/or run.

MOUNT ATTACKS

An alternative to standing up is to adopt the mount position and strike your opponent until he's out.

Sit on his torso so that you're facing him, and get your knees as far up towards his armpits as possible.

Use elbow strikes across his face/head, so that you won't smash your elbow into the ground if you miss.

You can choke him out by placing one arm under his neck. Grab your wrist with your other hand and squeeze tight so your shoulder and bicep cut of his blood supply. It will work better if his arm is between your head and his neck, as that will close the gap.

Alternatively, use your shoulder and opposite fist to squeeze on his arteries.

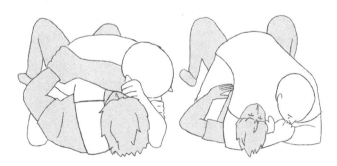

You can apply this from the side or from behind, on the ground or standing, though the RNC is more effective.

To learn more about ground fighting, visit:

www.SurvivalFitnessPlan.com/Ground-Fighting-Techniques

BLITZKRIEG

Blitzkrieg (lightning war) was a World War 2 military tactic that used surprise, speed, and an onslaught of concentrated firepower, with the aim of ending a battle as quickly as possible.

In this context, it means an onslaught of strikes to your opponent from all angles, and is a primary fighting strategy in a self-defense situation.

Make every strike as hard and fast as you can. Get in his space and claim it. Constantly push your opponent back and do not let up.

Use Blitzkrieg to overwhelm your opponent at close range, or as a complete start-to-finish fighting tactic. That is, start with long range strikes and keep closing in until he's down.

Constantly crowding your opponent in this way will unbalance him mentally and physically.

Example 1

- Low kick to knee
- Parry and strike
- Grab and elbow
- Simple trip
- Stomp

Example 2

- Elbow burst
- Multiple straight punches
- Knees to head
- Guillotine

Hitting the bag with blitzkrieg in sets (e.g., 30-second blitzkrieg, 10-second rest, 30-second blitzkrieg, and so on) makes a good fitness workout.

FEINTS

A feint is a false attack you can use to create an opening in which to strike.

Use a feint to land a blow when your opponent's defense is too good for your direct attacks.

Although there are many different ways to feint, the following simple ones are enough to outwit the average opponent for self-defense purposes.

High-High

Throw a lead straight to his head. As soon as he moves to parry, pull your hand back and then do a real strike in the opening that is created.

Low-High

Throw a low lead straight. As soon as he drops his guard to defend, pull your hand back and strike at his head.

IMMOBILIZATION ATTACKS

An immobilization attack (IA) prevents an opponent from moving a part of his body while you attack in the opening that is created.

Ideally, it forces an opening while keeping you protected from the body part(s) that you immobilize.

A basic IA is to use one hand to pin your opponent's arm (or arms) down while striking with your free arm.

In these two examples, the defender immobilizes the attacker's arm by grabbing it. He then pulls him in as he strikes his body.

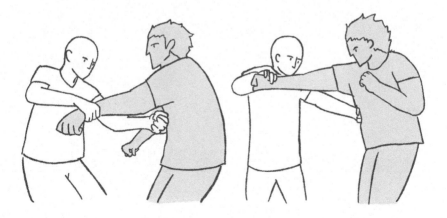

Immobilization is not limited to the hands. Arm-to-leg, leg-to-leg, head, and hair immobilization attacks are all possible.

Combining a feint with an immobilization attack works well.

For example, use a low-high feint. When your opponent drops his guard, pin his arms down and attack high.

WEAPON DISARMS

Weapon disarms are risky. To give yourself the best chance of success, get a weapon of your own first.

When you are disarmed and your opponent has a weapon, remember the following tips:

- A low side-kick can stun your opponent while keeping you out of striking range.
- Move hard and fast. Do not give him time to recover or change tactics.
- Keep your distance, and try to place stationary objects between the two of you.
- Watch the weapon and close in at an opportune moment.
- Expect to get injured, especially when fighting someone who has a knife.
- Whatever you choose to do, you must have conviction. Be all in or all out.

WEAPON VS WEAPON

If you're going to fight someone with a weapon, getting your own weapon will give you the best chance of success.

In addition to the following information, review the Improvised Weapons chapter.

Your opponent's hand makes a good secondary target if it's closer than his head.

When using a knife, use timing, footwork, and feints. Wait for your opponent to strike and then close in before he can recover. You can use a feint to time his strike.

If you have a club, use the overhead strike straight down along the central line. If your opponent uses an angled attack, your straight overhead will win. When you both use the overhead strike, the strike that hits its target first will succeed.

If your opponent's strike is going to beat yours, parry it. As his strike comes in, tap the top of your weapon on his to deflect it. Immediately return your club to the center line to finish your strike.

When you hold a longer weapon, keep the advantage of distance. Use footwork, overhead strikes, and thrusts.

LOW WEAPON DEFENSE

Only attempt an unarmed weapon disarm if you have no other choice —in a surprise attack, for example.

Even if you're well-trained, chances are you'll get injured. It's much safer to run, comply, or find your own weapon. However, when those options are not feasible, these techniques may save your life.

This specific technique is for any weapon attack that comes in below the 90-degree point of the attacker's elbow. The type of grip, the side, or the exact angle he strikes from don't matter.

Above 90 Degrees   Below 90 Degrees

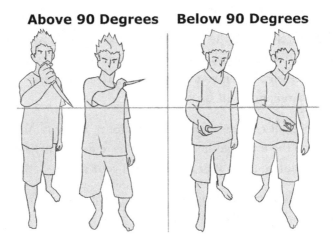

As the strike comes in, engage his arm with a cross-block. Point both your thumbs down so it's harder for the knife to slip through. Keep one hand high and one low to "surround" his elbow.

Push forward to prevent him from retracting the weapon.

Collapse into him as you redirect the weapon to the outside of your body

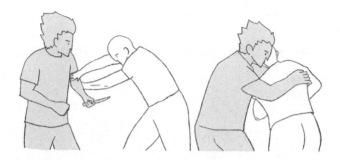

Wrap your arm around his tightly and immediately push him away as you scrape down his arm with your armpit.

You need to get below his elbow to minimize his range of motion with the knife.

Bring your fist to your chest to lock his arm using your armpit.

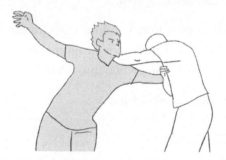

Apply upward pressure on his wrist until he lets go of the weapon.

Strike him if needed.

HIGH WEAPON DEFENSE

The high weapon defense is for any attack that comes from above the 90-degree point of the attacker's elbow.

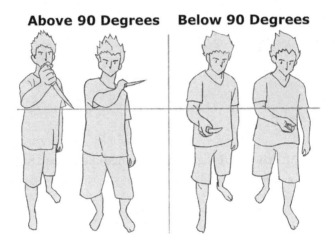

As the attack comes in, direct a modified elbow burst into the shoulder/upper part of his striking arm.

Modify it by having your lead hand on your forehead as opposed to the top of your head. This lowers your elbow so that you won't push him back as much when you collide into him.

Shove your arms over his shoulder.

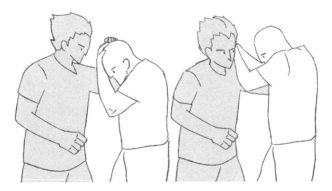

Wrap your arm around his tightly and immediately push him away as you scrape down his arm with your armpit.

Bring your fist to your chest to lock his arm using your armpit.

Apply slight upward pressure on his wrist until he lets go of the weapon.

Strike him if needed.

UNARMED GUN DEFENSE

This only works when you're within grabbing distance of the gun.

When you're six meters (20ft) or more away, run for cover using zigzag movements. If there is no cover, turn a corner as soon as possible.

When you're under 6 meters (20ft) away, but out of grabbing range, you're in the danger zone. Co-operate until an opportunity to run or disarm your opponent arises.

Note: If the assailant has a shotgun or rifle, his ability to accurately shoot increases to at least 50m (more for a rifle).

When you're within grabbing distance of the gun, it is possible to disarm your opponent. Consider the position of other people too.

Cover Vs Concealment

This is from the book *Evading and Escaping Capture*:

Concealment is anything between you and your opponent that hides you from sight.

Vegetation is a good method of concealment. The more of it there is between you and your opponent, the harder it will be for him to see you.

Cover will hide you from sight too, but will also stop bullets.

Many solid objects do not qualify as cover. Bullets will go through wooden fences, car doors, windows, etc.

Solid concrete, thick metal, depressions in the earth, and large trees have a much better chance of providing you cover. The more powerful the gun (or blast), the thicker the cover needs to be.

If your opponent is trying to shoot you, seek cover, but if they only want to find you, concealment is enough.

To learn more about escape and evasion, visit:

www.SurvivalFItnessPlan.com/Evading-Escaping-Capture

Front Gun Defense

Grab your opponent's hand and the body of the gun as you pivot out of the line of fire. It's best to do this when he's distracted.

Twist the weapon away from you and towards him, then pry it out of his hands.

As soon as you have the weapon, move away from him so he can't grab it back from you.

Check that the weapon is ready to fire, aim it at his torso, and warn him to stay back. if he approaches, fire.

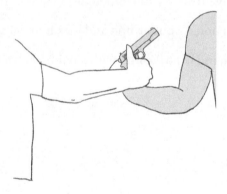

Rear Gun Defense

This is for if an attacker puts a gun to your back or the back of your head.

Put your hands up.

You want to get as close to the gun as possible, preferably so you can feel it. Try to feel which side the gun is on and which hand your opponent is holding it in. You may be able to see in a reflective surface in front of you. If you can't discern this, assume the gun is in his right hand.

Pivot in the opposite direction of the hand you think the gun is in, so you end up on the inside of you opponent's arm.

Capture his arm under your armpit and lock it in tight.

Use your other hand to strike him with a palm heel or elbow.

This can still work if you turn the wrong way, but it's more likely to work if you turn in towards him.

Continue to strike him until he's unconscious.

Rear Gun Defense 2

Here is an alternate gun defense for when your opponent grabs you (in a hostage situation, for example).

This only works if he has a loose hold on you. If you are held tight, wait until his grip loosens before attempting it.

Spin out of his grip and bring your arm underneath the one with which he's holding the gun.

Hook your arm under his and do a palm strike. Lock his wrist in the crook of your elbow by pinning your hand to your chest.

Pry the gun out of his hand as soon as you've hit your attacker. Point the nozzle towards him.

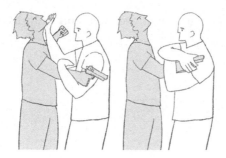

Doorway Gun Disarm

Use this tactic when hiding from an attacker on the other side of a door or around a corner.

As soon as you see the arm holding the weapon, grab onto the weapon and his arm with both hands.

Use your body weight to slam the weapon to the ground in front of you. Land on your knees if possible.

Pry the weapon out of his hand.

When there are two of you, stand one on each side of the door. Assign one person to the attacker's arm/weapon and one to his head. If there are three of you, the third person can go for his legs. Do not use more than three people to avoid getting in each other's way.

A better option is to get a weapon and smash it down on his hand/forearm.

MULTIPLE OPPONENTS

A second opponent is often more dangerous than a conventional weapon.

Three or more opponents become exceedingly dangerous due to their pack mentality.

Avoid being surrounded, and stay off the ground.

Use footwork and your surroundings to put yourself in advantageous positions:

- On higher ground
- With your back to the sun (so your opponents have to look into it)
- Behind obstacles

Staying in one spot is dangerous. Change your distance and angles continuously.

Line up your opponents using footwork and/or funneling.

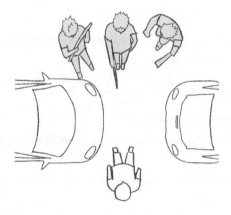

Head Control

A person will follow his head. With a modified guillotine or RNC (preferred), you can use one attacker as a human shield against the others.

Pin the hand of your choking arm to your chest (or hold your shirt) and hold him tightly, so you can use your other hand to fight the others.

Constantly move so he can't regain his balance.

When you have enough distance/time, you can choke him out.

When Surrounded

Pick a target and blitzkrieg him to break out of the circle.

In a "weak" group, such as a bunch of unorganized youths, taking out the leader may be enough to scare the others off. Be brutal, and tell his friends to take him to the hospital.

In other cases, when it seems all opponents are willing to fight, it may be better to break out through the weakest link, since that will be easier.

If they have weapons, always pick the least threatening person, in the following order of preference:

- No weapon
- Least dangerous weapon
- Best chance of overcoming (mentally and/or physically)

Once you're out of the "circle," run away or, if that isn't possible, turn to face your opponents.

Turning Strike

The turning strike is an alternative rear defense to the side kick.

To perform one, do a rear high elbow and then turn and face your opponent. Step back with the foot on the same side as your elbow.

As you turn, use a downward strike. Make contact with either your forearm or the back of your fist.

Continue your momentum, throwing a palm heel or rear straight punch.

Group Fighting Strategy

In this section, the first number indicated is your "team." For example, 2 VS 1 means two of you against one opponent.

Communication between team members is important to adapt to the situation, especially if one of you needs help.

2 VS 1

Advance together on either side of the enemy. As you close in, the person he isn't focused on should go for his legs, while the other concentrates on his upper body (or weapon).

3 VS 2

Advance and close so the outside two of you are to the outside of the enemy. Whoever is facing his opponent alone can fight or stall until the others have finished and can come to his aid.

Even Numbers

One fighter stays in reserve until the enemy has committed their entire force. The reserved fighter then attacks from behind.

2 VS 3

Both of you attack one opponent at a time until you have defeated all three. If you're separated, then Fighter 1 defends against two, while Fighter 2 fights one-on-one. Fighter 2 comes to Fighter 1's aid when he has finished with his own opponent.

COMPLIANCE LOCKS

Locks are not recommended for self-defense, but there may be a time when you want to escort someone out or hold someone in place until help arrives.

You could also use the wrist locks for disarms, but don't try to. Only use them if the opportunity presents itself while you're deploying one of the other weapon disarming techniques.

Wrist Locks

Place your thumbs together on the back of your opponent's hand, with the rest of your fingers are the palm side.

You can use a "wrist twist" to torque his wrist and forearm to the outside of his body.

Alternatively, force him down by torqueing it down.

For a "wrist lock," twist his wrist in towards his body.

Once his elbow is locked, apply pressure down and/or in towards him.

Notice the alternative to both thumbs on the outside. Instead, grab the thumb and wrist. Either way works for either wrist lock.

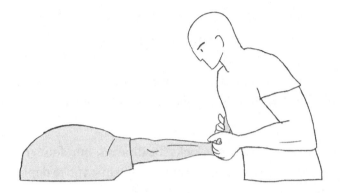

Arm Bar

This uses the same application as the RNC, but replaces your opponent's neck with his elbow.

If you do it while standing, you will be exposed to attack.

On the ground, place your knee on your opponent's torso or neck, and your other arm on his shoulder. This will give you more leverage and stability.

On the right is a variation of the arm bar. It also lets you demonstrate control by squeezing his neck between your legs.

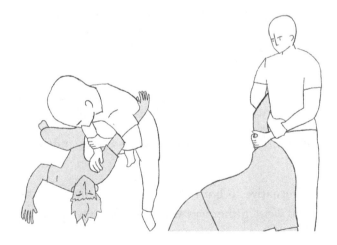

Dear Reader,

Thank you for reading *The Self-Defense Handbook*.

If you enjoyed it, please leave a review on Amazon. It helps more than most people think. You can do that here:

www.SurvivalFitnessPlan.com/Self-Defense-Handbook-Reviews

Claim your bonus materials:

www.SurvivalFitnessPlan.com/Free-Downloads

Connect with like-minded people and discuss anything SFP related via the SFP Facebook group:

www.Facebook.com/groups/SurvivalFitnessPlan

A list of resources used in the creation of the Self-Defense Series is available at:

www.SurvivalFitnessPlan.com/Self-Defense-Series

Thanks again for your support,

Sam Fury, Author.

AUTHOR RECOMMENDATIONS

Teach Yourself Jeet Kune Do!

Discover one of the most effective martial arts ever invented, because this is a complete training manual in Bruce Lee's Jeet Kune Do!

Get it now.

www.SurvivalFitnessPlan.com/Jeet-Kune-Do

Teach Yourself Escape and Evasion Tactics!

Discover the skills you need to evade and escape capture, because you never know when they will save your life!

Get it now.

www.SurvivalFitnessPlan.com/Evading-Escaping-Capture

SURVIVAL FITNESS PLAN TRAINING MANUALS

Survival Fitness

When in danger, you have two options: fight or flight.

This series contains training manuals on the best methods of flight. Together with self-defense, you can train in them for general health and fitness.

- **Parkour.** All the parkour skills you need to overcome obstacles in your path.
- **Climbing.** Focusing on essential bouldering techniques.
- **Riding.** Essential mountain-bike riding techniques. Go as fast as possible in the safest manner.
- **Swimming.** Swimming for endurance and/or speed using the most efficient strokes.

It also has books covering general health and wellness, such as yoga and meditation.

www.SurvivalFitnessPlan.com/Survival-Fitness-Series

Self-Defense

The Self-Defense Series has volumes on some of the martial arts used as a base in SFP self-defense.

It also contains the SFP self-defense training manuals. SFP Self-Defense is an efficient and effective form of minimalist self-defense.

www.SurvivalFitnessPlan.com/Self-Defense-Series

Escape, Evasion, and Survival

SFP escape, evasion, and survival (EES) focuses on keeping you alive using minimal resources. Subjects covered include:

- **Disaster Survival.** How to prepare for and react in the case of disaster and/or societal collapse.
- **Escape and Evasion.** The ability to escape capture and hide from your enemy.
- **Urban and Wilderness Survival.** Being able to live off the land in all terrains.
- **Emergency Roping.** Basic climbing skills and improvised roping techniques.
- **Water Rescue.** Life-saving water skills based on surf life-saving and military training course competencies.
- **Wilderness First Aid.** Modern medicine for use in emergency situations.
- **Sustainable Living.** Creating a lifestyle with minimal impact on the environment and maximum self-reliance.
- **Financial Freedom.** Long-term survival in the modern economic-based world.

www.SurvivalFitnessPlan.com/Escape-Evasion-Survival-Series

ABOUT THE AUTHOR

Sam Fury has had a passion for survival, evasion, resistance, and escape (SERE) training since he was a young boy growing up in Australia.

This led him to years of training and career experience in related subjects, including martial arts, military training, and outdoor pursuits.

These days, he spends his time refining his skills and sharing what he learns via his books and blog.

www.SurvivalFitnessPlan.com

facebook.com/SurvivalFitnessPlan

twitter.com/Survival_Fitnes

pinterest.com/survivalfitnes

goodreads.com/SamFury

bookbub.com/authors/sam-fury

amazon.com/author/samfury

Made in the USA
Monee, IL
02 September 2020